Boyfriends
+
Girlfriends

Boyfriends
+
Girlfriends

A Guide to Dating for People with Disabilities

Terri Couwenhoven, M.S.

Woodbine House

Library of Congress Cataloging-in-Publication Data

Couwenhoven, Terri.
  Boyfriends & girlfriends : a guide to dating for people with disabilities / by
Terri Couwenhoven. -- First edition.
      pages cm
  Includes bibliographical references and index.
  ISBN 978-1-60613-255-5 (pbk. : alk. paper) 1. People with disabilities--
Sexual behavior. 2. Dating (Social customs) 3. Man-woman relationships.
4. Sex instruction for people with disabilities. I. Title. II. Title: Boyfriends and
girlfriends.
  HQ30.5.C68 2015
  306.73--dc23

                                                              2015016161

Manufactured in the United States of America

10 9 8 7 6 5 4

Table of Contents

Introduction

This book is about boyfriends, girlfriends, and dating...but it's also about *real life*. The boyfriends and girlfriends you see on TV, in movies, or on the Internet are not always real. Often they are actors who have roles to play. This book is about what *real people* who are dating do in *real life*.

This book explains how to start a relationship with a boyfriend or girlfriend—if that is something that you want. If you already have a boyfriend or girlfriend, this book will help you learn about healthy relationships. That way you can enjoy a dating relationship that is safe and fun.

This book probably won't answer *every* question you have about dating. But it should help you understand the most important facts about starting or improving a girlfriend/boyfriend relationship. If you still have questions after finishing this book, be sure to talk with a parent, teacher, staff person, or another adult you trust.

Best wishes for a healthy and happy relationship!

CHAPTER 1

Dating Basics

WHAT IS A DATE?

Going on a "date" means you plan to spend time with someone you like or are interested in. And… the person you plan to spend time with…likes and is interested in you too!

 ### ACTIVITY: DATE QUIZ

1. You go out with a group of friends to the movies. Is this a date? **YES / NO**

2. You plan some time with your cousin. Is this a date? **YES / NO**

3. You plan to go to a dance with a person you have a crush on. Is this a date? **YES / NO**

4. You go out with your family for dinner. Is this a date? **YES / NO**

5. Someone you have a crush on sits next to you at school. Is this a date? **YES / NO**

A little tricky, right? Only number 3 is a real date. That's because three things must be true for it to be a date:

1. You and the other person *both* agree and plan to spend time together.

2. The other person is not a relative (cousin, brother or sister, parent, etc.).

3. You are both attracted to each other.

 A **date** is a planned get-together between two people who might like to be boyfriend/girlfriend or are already a couple.

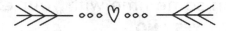

WHY DO PEOPLE DATE?

Dating is the main way couples get to know each other. If two people like each other, spending time together is the best way to learn about each other. When couples spend time together, it helps them decide if they are a good match for each other.

Dating can also be a lot of fun. You can do and see things together that you both enjoy. This can help you find out if you like doing the same things.

DATING DETAIL

People date so they can see if they are a good match for each other. If two people are a good match, a boyfriend/girlfriend relationship can start. Two people who are dating are called a **couple.**

ARE YOU OLD ENOUGH TO DATE?

People are ready for dating at different ages.

18? 16? 20? 25? 40?

Most people don't start dating until they are in high school. Many people don't feel ready to date until they are out of school and are adults. Some people don't date until they meet the right person, and sometimes that takes a while. And others are just not interested in dating. All of these choices are okay.

ARE YOU READY TO DATE?

Being ready to date is more than just being the right age. To be ready to date, you also need these skills:

- ♥ You know how to handle yourself around others.

- ♥ You know how to act like an adult, be polite, and treat others respectfully.

- ♥ You can care about someone else as much as you care about yourself.

- ♥ You know how to stay safe and speak up for yourself.

If you want to begin dating, talk to the people you live with about it. They may have rules about dating. They may want you to be a certain age to date. Or maybe they want you to know how to do certain things like use a cell phone.

Sometimes parents and support people worry a lot about safety. Let them know that you understand their concerns. But ask them to help you learn the skills that will help you be ready to date. See Chapter 4 for ideas on how to date safely.

Take the **Dating Readiness Quiz** on the next page!

DATING READINESS QUIZ

	No	I'm Learning	Yes
I can speak up for myself.	☐	☐	☐
I have good manners.	☐	☐	☐
I let others know how I feel.	☐	☐	☐
I wait my turn.	☐	☐	☐
I don't interrupt.	☐	☐	☐
I listen well.	☐	☐	☐
I don't always have to have my way.	☐	☐	☐
I know how to stay safe.	☐	☐	☐
I know how to take turns.	☐	☐	☐
I can share with others.	☐	☐	☐

Other things I would like to learn: _____

_____

_____

_____

_____

CHAPTER 2

Sexual Feelings and Crushes

If you want to have a boyfriend or girlfriend, you need to know about two things first:

- ♥ sexual feelings

- ♥ crushes

Both of these things are a *big* part of boyfriend/girlfriend relationships.

WHAT ARE SEXUAL FEELINGS?

Have you ever noticed the feelings you get inside your body when you see or think about a person you like?

- ♥ Your stomach might flutter a bit.

♥ Maybe your heart beats faster.

♥ Your hands might get sweaty.

♥ You feel nervous when you see or are close to the person.

♥ You think about how it might feel to touch or kiss the person or be touched or kissed by him or her.

These feelings inside your body are called *sexual feelings.* If you notice sexual feelings when you are with someone, it does *not* mean you can kiss, hug, or touch the person. It does *not* mean you can or should have sex with the person.

Sexual feelings are a way your body lets you know that you like someone. Sexual feelings are normal and happen to everyone.

WHAT IS A CRUSH?

When you have sexual feelings for a person it's called *"having a crush."* Sometimes it's also called *"being attracted to"* or *"liking"* someone.

Having a crush on someone does not mean that the person is your boyfriend or girlfriend. It just means you have strong feelings for that person.

Sometimes the person you like has a crush on you too. Sometimes he or she doesn't. (See "One-Way Crushes" on the next page.)

If you are looking for someone to date, it helps to figure out who you like and why you like them. Most people only date people they like or are interested in.

 ACTIVITY: WHO DO YOU LIKE?

1. Do you have a crush on somebody?   **YES / NO**

2. What happens inside your body when you see or are close to the person you like?

   _____

   _____

3. What are some reasons you like this person?

_____

_____

If you do not have a crush right now, that is okay. Not everyone has a crush. Maybe you just haven't found a person you are interested in yet.

HANDLING SEXUAL FEELINGS & CRUSHES

It is important for teens and adults to know:

1. what to do with your sexual feelings and

2. how to handle crushes.

Just because you like someone does not mean you can kiss, touch, or hug the person. You have to pay attention to how the other person feels.

One-Way Crushes

Sometimes a person *you* have a crush on *does not feel the same way about you.* This happens a lot. The other person might like you as a friend, but not as a boyfriend/girlfriend. Or he or she might not care about you at all.

If someone you like does not feel the same way about you, what should you do?

- ♥ You can still talk to them and be around them. It feels good to be close to people we like.

- ♥ Enjoy your sexual feelings, but keep them to yourself.

- ♥ Do not tell the person you love him or her.

- ♥ Do not call the person your boyfriend or girlfriend.

- ♥ And do not try to kiss or hug him or her.

You can be friends with the person—just not boyfriend/girlfriend. A boyfriend/girlfriend relationship cannot start unless *two* people like *each other*.

 Having sexual feelings or crushes is normal. When you have a crush on someone who does not feel the same way about you, it is best to keep your sexual feelings to yourself.

Only one person has a crush.
Can you guess which one?

See page 28 for signs that someone might not be interested in you.

Two-Way Crushes

Sometimes you can have a crush on someone and *he or she likes you too*! This means you have sexual feelings for each other. When this happens, you both feel like you want to be more than friends. This is one way boyfriend/girlfriend relationships can start.

See page 28 for signs that someone might have a crush on you.

A two-way crush is one way a boyfriend/girlfriend relationship can start.

What Does It Mean If Someone Is Gay?

Being gay means a person gets crushes on people of the same gender. Men who have crushes on other men are gay. They are not interested in dating women. Women who get crushes on other women are gay. They are not interested in dating men. Another word for gay is *homosexual*.

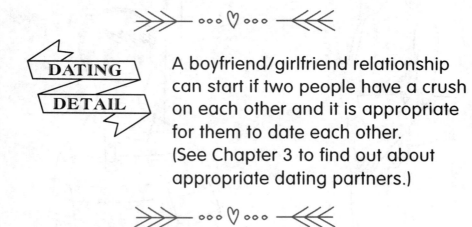

DATING DETAIL

A boyfriend/girlfriend relationship can start if two people have a crush on each other and it is appropriate for them to date each other.
(See Chapter 3 to find out about appropriate dating partners.)

Let's talk more about boyfriends, girlfriends, and dating.

Starting a Boyfriend/Girlfriend Relationship

Boyfriend/girlfriend relationships don't just happen. You need to do some things to get started. This section will help you learn the steps you need to take to start a boyfriend/girlfriend relationship.

STEP 1: FIND SOMEONE WHO INTERESTS YOU

The first step in starting a boyfriend/girlfriend relationship is finding someone you like or are interested in getting to know better. This is the hardest step for most people.

First, here are some rules about finding someone to date.

People Who Are Off-Limits

Family Members:

Family members are people who are related to you in some way. Parents, cousins, step-brothers, step-sisters, aunts, uncles, and grandparents are family members. When a brother or sister gets married, their husbands or wives become part of your family too.

It is not okay to date family members. People in your family cannot be your boyfriend or girlfriend.

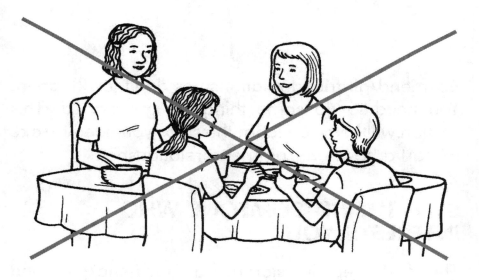

Paid Helpers:

People in your life who are paid to help or support you are called *paid helpers*.

- Your teacher is paid to help you learn new things. You cannot date your teacher.

- Your job coach is paid to help you find a job and teach you how to do your job. You cannot date your job coach.

- If you live in an apartment or group home, there might be staff who are paid to help you take care of yourself and stay safe. You cannot date staff.

- Doctors, nurses, and therapists are off limits too.

Children or Minors:
If you are 18 years old or older, you are an adult. In most states, it is against the law for adults to date people younger than 18. If you are an adult, make sure you only date other adults. Do not date children who are 17 or younger.

If you are 17 or younger, you should not be dating adults. Teens under 18 usually date other teenagers. So, look for someone about the same age as you.

People Who Already Have Boyfriends or Girlfriends:

The person you date has to be *single*. Being single means the person is not married or dating anyone else. When you are looking for someone to date, make sure they are single and not already in a boyfriend/girlfriend relationship.

Sometimes people have crushes on family members, paid helpers, or people who already have a boyfriend or girlfriend. That is okay, but it is best to keep your sexual feelings private. Telling these people how you feel can make them uncomfortable. These are people you cannot date. They cannot be your boyfriend or girlfriend.

Ideas for Finding Someone to Date

Sometimes it can be really hard to find someone to date! If you want to start a boyfriend/girlfriend relationship, here are some common ways people find someone to date.

Friends:

Do you have friends who are fun and like to do things you like to do? Sometimes friends can turn into boyfriends or girlfriends if both people want that to happen.

Groups or Clubs:

One good way to meet someone is to spend time with people who like to do the same things you like. When two people have things in common, it is easier to start a relationship. Joining clubs, sports teams like Special Olympics, or self-advocacy groups like People First are ways to meet people. What groups do you belong to?

Friends of Friends:

Sometimes we meet people through our friends. When you don't know a person very well but a friend does, your friend can help you learn about the person. A friend can help you decide if you have things in common or if you might be a good match.

Other Ideas:

Try taking a class that interests you. Do you like art? Theater? Karate? Dancing? Cooking? Yoga? How about a computer or sign language class? Or an exercise class? Going to conferences is a good way to meet people too.

Volunteering for a group you care about is another good way to meet new people! Do you care about the environment? You could volunteer to help clean up a park or pull weeds. Do you want to help other people? You could volunteer at a hospital or retirement home. What do you care about the most?

Not-So-Safe Ways to Meet People to Date

On the Internet:

When you meet people online, it is hard to know if they are good people. People online can lie about who they are because you can't see them. They might pretend they are a different age or that they really like you when they do not. This happens a lot.

It is hard to know the truth about people you meet online, so the Internet is not the best place to meet a person to date.

There are some dating sites just for people with disabilities. (See page 113.) But be careful if you

I'm a
19 y.o
female

use them. If you are using the Internet, do not give out private information about yourself to people you "meet" online. Do not tell them where you live or your phone number. Do not send strangers a picture of you, either.

In Public Places

It is not a good idea to try to find a girlfriend or boyfriend on the bus, in malls, in parks, or in bars. When you look for a person to date in these places, it makes you look *desperate*. Being desperate means you will date anyone without knowing anything about them. This isn't safe. Other people can tell when you are desperate. If a stranger sees that you are desperate, he or she might pretend to like you so you will do whatever he or she wants you to do.

At Work:

When you are at work, it is important to do your job. Your boss will be upset if you spend your time trying to find someone to date. Also, looking for a boyfriend or girlfriend at work can make your coworkers uncomfortable. They need to be able to work with you in a business-like way. That is impossible if you are trying to flirt with them. (See pages 26-27 for information on flirting.)

What If I Can't Find Anyone?

Finding a person who interests you can be hard. If you are having problems, here are some things you can do:

- *Get out of the house!* It's hard to meet new people if you spend your free time at home. Being with friends in the community and doing things that are interesting is a good first step for finding someone.

- *Join new groups!* Look for new groups to join. If you always see the same people, you may have to join new groups to meet new people.

- *Present your best self!* First impressions are important. Make sure you look your best when you are around others. Use your manners. Be respectful. You never know when you might meet someone. And when you do, you want to be at your best!

- **_Expand your circle of friends!_** If you live in a small town, the number of people you could date might be very small. Try to find state or national groups to join so you can meet new people. Go to conventions. Or, do you have some old friends you liked but don't see very often? Try getting back in touch with them to see if you could get together.

- **_Be open to all possibilities!_** Try not to get stuck on who you will or will not date. For example, don't decide you will only date people who do not have a disability or who look a certain way. This makes it much harder to find someone. How someone looks is only a small part of who a person is. You might miss out on a person who is caring, has a good heart, or has a great sense of humor.

Remember, just because you like someone's looks doesn't mean you will get along. If you don't have anything in common, it is hard to keep a relationship going.

DATING DETAIL Boyfriend/girlfriend relationships work out better when two people have things in common.

STEP 2: SEE IF THE PERSON YOU LIKE IS INTERESTED IN YOU!

After you see or meet someone you like, you have to *do something* to let the person know you are interested. This is called *flirting*. Flirting means you *send signals* to the person you like. The signals you send can help the person know you are interested.

Let the Person Know You Are Interested: Send Signals

It's important to let the person know you are interested in him or her. If the person doesn't know you like him or her, a dating relationship might never start.

Here are some ways to send signals to let someone know you are interested in him or her:

♥ **Flirt with Your Body:**
- ➻ Lean in and move close to the person (no touching).
- ➻ Make eye contact.
- ➻ Nod and smile to show you are interested in what the person is saying.

♥ **Flirt with Words:**
- ➻ If you are meeting someone for the first time, introduce yourself.

➤ Let the person know you are happy to see him or her. You could say something like this:

- "I'm happy you came."
- "I was hoping you'd be here."
- "Great to see you again."

➤ Give the person a *compliment*. A compliment means you say something that will make the person feel good. You could say something like this:

- "You look nice tonight."
- "You are a great dancer."
- "I love your smile."

Try not to get too personal when you are talking to the person you like. Do not say things like "I love your big boobs" or "You are hot and I want to have sex with you." Personal remarks can stop people from wanting to be your girlfriend or boyfriend. Saying things that are private can make people feel uncomfortable.

Decide If the Person Is Interested in You: Reading Signals

After you send your signals, you need to pay close attention. Watch the person to see if he or she sends signals back. The signals the person sends back help you know if you should keep flirting or stop.

♥ *Signals that the Person Might Be Interested:*
➤ The person stays and talks to you.
➤ The person is smiling and seems to enjoy talking to you.
➤ He or she seems to want to keep the conversation going.
➤ He or she makes eye contact with you. (If the person has autism, he or she might not do this.)

♥ *Signals That You Should Stop Flirting:*
➤ The person keeps walking away from you.
➤ He or she doesn't look happy to be near you.
➤ He or she avoids you. (If the person sees you coming, he or she goes in another direction.)
➤ The person doesn't look at you when he or she talks to you. (Remember, though: someone with autism might not make eye contact but still like you.)
➤ The person answers you very briefly with no interest in his or her voice.
➤ The person seems more interested in talking with other people than with you.

ACTIVITY:
Interested or Not Interested?
What Do You Think?

Instructions: Look at the people in the pictures below. Look for body signals that help you know if the people are interested or not interested in each other.

Which people are flirting (interested)? Which people are sending signals that they are *not* interested?

Flirting with People with Autism

It can be hard for people with autism to make eye contact. If you have autism and eye contact is hard for you, try to use all the other signals to show you are interested in someone. If you're flirting with someone who might have autism, don't assume the person doesn't like you *just* because of lack of eye contact. Look for other signals that tell you the person is interested.

If the person you are flirting with does not seem interested, stop flirting! A boyfriend/girlfriend relationship can't start unless **both** people are interested in each other.

Other Flirting Rules

♥ If someone is flirting with you and you are *not interested*, let the person know right away. Send clear signals you are not interested. You could turn your back or walk away. Or you could say, "I have to go" or "I have a call I have to take." Flirting can be fun, but it's mean to pretend you are interested when you are not.

♥ If you already have a boyfriend or girlfriend, do not flirt with anybody else. If you are not happy in your relationship, try fixing the problems (pages 60-65) or break up (Chapter 8). Most people date one person at a time.

♥ If someone is flirting with you but you are already dating someone, be honest. You could say, "I'm already dating someone" or "I'm not available right now" or "I'm taken." Most people only date one person at a time.

♥ There are times when flirting is not okay. Do not flirt if you are too young to date or if you are supposed to be learning or working. It's also not okay to flirt with teachers or family, or while you are on the job.

Flirting is not a game. Flirting is for people who are old enough to date, are single, and are interested in starting a boyfriend/girlfriend relationship.

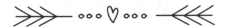

STEP 3: SPEND TIME GETTING TO KNOW EACH OTHER — DATE!

When you find someone you like and he or she is also interested in you, you can move to step 3... spending time getting to know each other.

Some couples text or talk on the phone when they first meet. This is one way to learn about the person you like.

At some point, it is important to spend time together in person. *Dating* is the main way couples spend time together. Going on a date means the two of you plan to do something together that you will both enjoy. Being together is the only way to decide if you are a good match for each other and if the person is safe.

Asking Someone to Go on a Date

Asking someone out on a date is private. Try to find a quiet place when the person is alone and not near friends or other people. Don't ask during class or while you are both working.

If it's not easy to get the person alone, you can call or text him or her instead. You could say, "Would you like to go out sometime?" or "Can we get together sometime?

It takes some courage to ask a person you like on a date. Some people are shy. Nowadays, a man or a woman can do the asking.

You can't force a person to like you. If the person you ask on a date says no, it's best to try to find someone else. Don't give up! It takes time to find the right person.

What If the Person You Ask Says No?

Ouch! Hearing someone say no can hurt, but it happens a lot. Sometimes it's hard to read somebody's signals, or his or her signals aren't clear. If the person says no, respect his or her feelings and move on. A boyfriend/girlfriend relationship can't start unless both people are interested in each other.

What If Someone Asks You Out and You're Not Interested?

You have the right to decide what you want to do. That includes turning down an invitation to go out. It's best to say no if you are not interested in the person or don't feel safe.

If you're not sure how you feel, you could try one or two dates. Then see what you learn about the person. Talk to a family member or support person if you're not sure what to do.

What If the Person You Ask Says Yes?

YEAH! If you both agree to go out, you can start planning a time to get together. If you are new at dating, get some advice from your family or the people you live with. They can help with planning if you get stuck. Here are things to think about:

How to Plan a Date: Where Can We Go? What Can We Do?

When you go on a date there are things you need to think about. Talk to the people you live with so they can help. Here are some things to think about:

- ♥ Pick a day and time that works for both of you.

- ♥ Figure out what you can afford and who will pay. This helps you both know how much money to bring.

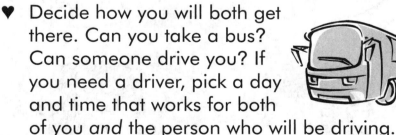

- ♥ Decide how you will both get there. Can you take a bus? Can someone drive you? If you need a driver, pick a day and time that works for both of you *and* the person who will be driving.

- ♥ If you already know the person well, pick an activity you know your date will enjoy.

If you don't know the person very well, plan a safe date.

Here are ways you can plan to be safe:

♥ Try group dating! A group date means one or two other dating couples or friends go on the date together. This way you can learn about the person while being with other friends you know and trust.

♥ Pick a public place to meet. If you don't know the person very well, limit the time you are alone or in private. Try meeting at a restaurant, theater, coffee shop, or mall. That way you can talk with your date but other people are around. Don't let the person know where you live until you know you can trust him or her.

♥ Use a chaperone. A *chaperone* is a person who stays nearby in case you need help. A chaperone could be any adult you trust: a parent, adult brother or sister, or support person. Chaperones are a good idea if you are just learning how to date or don't know much about the person you are dating.

♥ Plan a shorter date. Plan to do something that will not take much time: bowling one game, having a cup of coffee, or meeting at a theater to see a movie. As you learn more about the person, you can decide if you feel safe spending more time with him or her.

Getting Ready for Your Date

It's important to look and feel your best when you are on a date with someone you like.

♥ Make sure you look and smell good.

♥ Shower, shave, and brush your teeth and hair.

♥ Choose clothes that match what you will be doing on your date. (Don't wear a prom dress with high heels or a suit and tie if you're going to a movie or bowling.)

♥ Make sure your clothes are clean and you look your best!

Other things you can do:

♥ Make sure you have emergency phone numbers in your cell phone.

♥ Figure out how much money you will need, and then bring a little extra.

♥ If you're taking public transportation, find out the nearest stop to where you will be going. Figure out when you need to catch the bus or subway to arrive on time.

On the Date

Remember, people go on dates to get to know each other and have fun! One way to do that is to ask questions and then listen to your date's answers. Here are some questions to get you started:

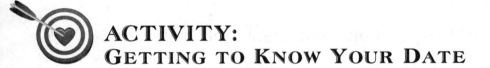

ACTIVITY: GETTING TO KNOW YOUR DATE

Questions for a date *you don't know very well:*

♥ Where did you grow up?

♥ How do you like to spend your day?

♥ What do you like to do for fun?

♥ Do you work? What do you do?

♥ Do you have hobbies?

♥ What is your family like?

♥ Who is your favorite singer?

♥ What kinds of movies do you like to watch?

♥ Can you think of other questions that would help you learn more about your date?

Fun questions for a date *you know pretty well*:

♥ If you could go anywhere in the world, where would you go?

♥ If you had a million dollars, what would you buy?

♥ What would your dream job be?

♥ What famous person would you most like to meet?

Can you think of other questions that would be fun to talk about?

Touch and Affection on Your First Date

One of the special things about dating is sharing touch and affection.

For more information on sharing touch and affection, go to the next chapter.

CHAPTER 4

Sharing Touch and Affection

Boyfriends and girlfriends can do many things to show that they care about each other. They say nice things to each other. They call or text to make sure the other person is okay. They talk to each other about their day. Or they do things to make the other person smile.

Sharing touch and affection is another way couples show that they care about each other. Sharing touch and showing affection is something that makes boyfriend/girlfriend relationships special.

DATING DETAIL

Sharing touch and affection is one of the special things about boyfriend/ girlfriend relationships.

TYPES OF TOUCH AND AFFECTION

Here are some common ways couples share touch and affection when they are *just getting to know each other*.

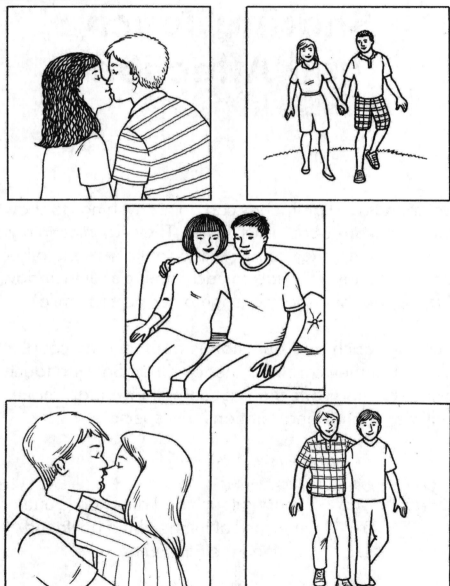

Most of these types of touch and affection are okay in public. But keep the hugging and kissing short if you are in public.

DATING DETAIL Boyfriends and girlfriends who don't know each other very well share less touch and affection than couples who do know each other well.

RULES FOR SHARING TOUCH AND AFFECTION

Know Your Boundaries

Your *boundary* is a line that others cannot cross without your permission. If you are dating someone, you need to know what kinds of touch and affection feel okay and not okay for YOU! Knowing your boundaries means you know what you will and will not do on a date.

For example, it might take a few months before you feel ready to kiss your boyfriend or girlfriend. But you might really like holding hands or sitting close with your arms around each other. Another person might feel ready to kiss the first or second time they go out on a date. Lines, or boundaries, can be different for different people.

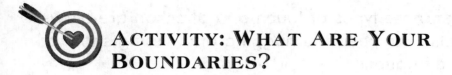

ACTIVITY: WHAT ARE YOUR BOUNDARIES?

You need to decide for yourself what your boundaries are. Ask yourself:

1. Is it OK for my boyfriend/girlfriend to hold my hand?

Yes   **No**

2. Is it OK for my boyfriend/girlfriend to give me a hug?

Yes   **No**

3. Is it OK for us to sit with our arms around each other?

Yes   **No**

4. Is it OK for us to walk with our arms around each other?

Yes   **No**

5. Is it OK for him/her to kiss me on the cheek?

Yes   **No**

6. Is it OK for him/her to kiss me on the lips?

Yes   **No**

7. Is it OK for our tongues to touch when we kiss?

Yes   **No**

If you don't like certain types of touch and affection, it is okay to say "I don't like that" or "I don't feel ready", or "stop".

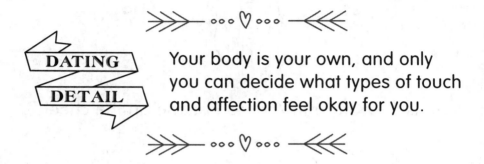

DATING DETAIL Your body is your own, and only you can decide what types of touch and affection feel okay for you.

Your Partner's Boundaries

It is perfectly normal for two people to feel differently about being touched. Often, boyfriends and girlfriends are ready for different kinds of touch and affection at different times. When this happens, you need to understand each other's *boundaries*.

Respect Your Partner's Boundaries

Your date has boundaries (lines) too! And his or her lines can be different than yours. For example, you might like light, tickly touches, but your boyfriend/girlfriend does not. Or you might want to "French kiss," but your date doesn't want to.

If your boyfriend/girlfriend tells you he or she does not like certain types of touch or affection, don't try this with him or her. If your date pushes you away or moves away, it means he or she wants to stop. Stop what you are doing if your date says, "I don't like that" or "I don't feel ready" or "stop."

It is never okay to make boyfriends/girlfriends do something they don't want to do. Respect your partner's boundaries: stop when your date says stop. It shows that you care about your date when you stop doing something he or she doesn't like.

Talk about What You Like and Don't Like

When you are getting to know someone, it can be hard to talk about affection you like and don't like. It gets easier to talk about touch as you spend more time together.

It is a good idea to ask first before you try new types of touch with your date. You could say "How about a kiss?" or "Would you like a back rub?" Asking permission shows you are respecting boundaries.

DATING DETAIL Talking about touches you like and don't like is something dating couples do.

Having Boundary Problems?

Here are some ways to tell that your boundaries are not being respected.

You feel pressure to change your boundaries.
Pressure means you feel pushed to do sexual things you don't want to do. Your date might use words to make you feel like you should give in. Pressure might sound like this:

- ♥ "If you loved me you would...."

- ♥ "I'll break up with you if you don't...."

- ♥ "Don't you care about me?"

- ♥ "This is what all boyfriends/girlfriends do."

Your boyfriend or girlfriend doesn't listen when you say no
What if you tell your date no and he or she doesn't listen? That means he or she is not respecting your

boundaries. This is not okay. Your body is your own, and you get to decide what feels safe.

DATING DETAIL
Your body is your own. You have the right to feel safe in your relationship. It is never okay for your date to pressure you to change your boundaries if you are not ready.

ACTIVITY: DO YOU RESPECT BOUNDARIES?

1. Do you stop when you hear the word "no" or "stop"? **YES / NO**

2. Do you use pressure to get your date to change his or her mind about doing sexual things (kissing or other types of touch)? **YES / NO**

3. Do you try to control your boyfriend or girlfriend? **YES / NO**

If you answered yes to question 1 and no to questions 2 and 3, you probably respect boundaries. If your answers were different, you need to work more on respecting your date's boundaries.

CHAPTER 5

How Are Things Going?

When you have a boyfriend or girlfriend, you should take the time to think about your relationship now and then. Is it a good relationship that you want to continue? Or do you have some concerns about it? This brings us to Step 4:

STEP 4: EVALUATING YOUR RELATIONSHIP

Dating helps you get to know a person better. After a few dates, you may start to feel different about him or her.

There are three things that can happen after you spend time dating someone…

Option 1: Your Feelings for Each Other Get Stronger

This can happen when two people are a good match for each other. Being a good match means you have things in common and enjoy being together. It feels good to find someone you really like and who likes you.

If you both think you are a good match for each other, you might decide to be a "couple" or "boyfriend/ girlfriend." This means you decide together that you will only date each other and nobody else. This is sometimes called "going steady" or "being a couple."

Being a couple can mean many things. It does not necessarily mean you are going to get engaged or married. It just means that you are a good match for each other, and for now, you have decided to only date each other and nobody else.

Often, things don't change much when you become a couple. Your relationship may stay exactly the same. But there might be little changes like these:

♥ You spend more time together dating.

♥ You are more comfortable with each other.

♥ You want to try different kinds of touch and affection or have sex.

Boyfriends/girlfriends still break up sometimes (see Chapter 8). And sometimes two people who have been boyfriend/girlfriend for many years decide they want to get more serious with each other. See Chapter 9 on serious relationships.

DATING DETAIL

Being boyfriend/girlfriend or a "couple" means you both agree to date each other and nobody else.

Option 2: You Are Not Sure How You Feel

What if you go on a couple dates with someone but you're not sure how you feel about him or her?

It takes time to really get to know someone. It can take more than one or two dates to decide if you are a good match for each other.

If you are not sure how you feel about the person, you can keep dating him or her and see if your feelings change. Or you can stop dating and start over with someone else. (Go back to Step 1 on page 17.)

Option 3: You Lose Interest or Want to Stop Dating

Sometimes after you date somebody a while, you learn things that make you lose interest in him or her. And you want to stop dating.

Not all boyfriend/girlfriend relationships work out. It can take many tries to find the right person. See the next page for some common reasons relationships don't work out.

TYPES OF RELATIONSHIPS THAT DON'T WORK OUT

There are dozens of reasons why boyfriend/ girlfriend relationships fail. Here are a few of the more common ones.

1. The "It's all about me" relationship

A dating relationship is about *two* people, not just one. When one person cares only about himself or herself, it is hard to keep a relationship going.

2. The "I can't breathe" relationship

Sometimes a boyfriend or girlfriend can take way too much time and work. Even if you are dating someone, you still get to spend time with family and friends, at work or at school. You still have a life! When one person takes too much time and work, sometimes couples break up.

3. The "space invader" relationship

Some people think that they get to touch their boyfriend or girlfriend any way they want to. But people don't feel respected if they are forced or pressured to do sexual things that they don't want to do. This can cause break-ups.

4. The "I'm the boss" relationship

Sometimes it can feel like one person in a relationship has all the power. This can make the other person feel like he or she has no power. In healthy relationships, couples take turns making decisions and sharing ideas. Break-ups can happen if one person is bossy and always controls the other person.

On Friday we are going to a party. You need to take off work. Call me when you get home.

You're not the boss of me!

DATING DETAIL

Spending time with someone helps you decide if you are a good match for each other. Not all people you date will be a good match for you. It can take many tries to find the right person.

CHAPTER 6

Fixing Problems

It is normal for all dating couples to have problems now and then. Fixing problems is part of the work of being in a boyfriend/girlfriend relationship. If you and your boyfriend/girlfriend are having problems, you can try to see if the problem is fixable.

IS THE PROBLEM FIXABLE?

Sometimes a problem is *not* fixable. For example, you and your date might have different personalities that do not work well together. That could make it too hard for you to get along. The last chapter included some examples of couples whose personalities just did not match.

A problem also might not be fixable if you do not feel safe or respected when you are with your boyfriend or girlfriend. This is a very serious problem. It is discussed in Chapter 7.

Chapter 7 also discusses some other problems that might not be fixable.

FIXING PROBLEMS

All couples run into problems when they are dating. And many problems *are* fixable. If you and your boyfriend or girlfriend are having a problem, try following the steps below.

1.) *Figure out what the problem is.*
First, try to be very clear about the problem. Be as specific as possible. For example:

NOT HELPFUL	MORE HELPFUL
She's avoiding me.	She never calls me back.
He's being mean.	He flirts with other girls.
She doesn't like me anymore.	We hardly see each other.

2.) Talk with your boyfriend/girlfriend about the problem.

Politely tell him or her what the problem is. It can help to start your sentence with "I."

3.) *Listen to what your partner has to say.*

LESS HELPFUL

Stop calling me so much!

MORE HELPFUL

I can't answer my phone while I'm at work.

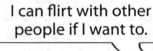

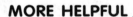

LESS HELPFUL

I can flirt with other people if I want to.

MORE HELPFUL

I'm sorry. I didn't realize that.

LESS HELPFUL

I don't have time to talk right now.

MORE HELPFUL

After play practice I will have more time to be with you.

4.) Talk about ways the problem can be handled.

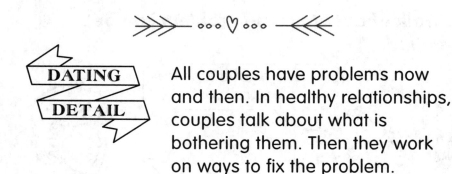

DATING DETAIL

All couples have problems now and then. In healthy relationships, couples talk about what is bothering them. Then they work on ways to fix the problem.

5.) *Ask for help if you need it.*
A parent, brother or sister, or staff person might have advice about problems you are having with your boyfriend/girlfriend.

Solving problems can be hard. When there is a problem, try something! If you just ignore the problem, it will *not* go away.

Need some practice solving problems? Go to the Dating Dilemma section on page 103. Look at the common problems and see if you can solve them.

Sometimes when couples work on their problems, things get better. Other times the problems are too big to fix. Problems that are too big to fix can lead to breakups. See Chapter 8.

CHAPTER 7

Do You Feel Respected?

You have the right to feel cared for and respected in dating relationships. Being respected means you are sure your boyfriend/girlfriend is kind to you, cares about your feelings, and does not hurt you. Being treated with respect helps people feel safe. Feeling safe means you trust your date to do the right thing.

There is only one way to decide if someone is safe and can be trusted: watch what the person **does** over time. What people **do** (**not** what they say) shows you if they are safe and can be trusted.

When you first meet someone, there is no way to know if he or she is safe or can be trusted. Deciding if a person is safe takes time. You have to pay close attention to how the person treats you and how he or she treats others *while you are together*.

SIGNS YOUR RELATIONSHIP IS UNHEALTHY

Sometimes a relationship needs to end because it is unhealthy. An *unhealthy relationship* means someone is doing something that is hurtful, unsafe, or against the law.

If you have a boyfriend or girlfriend, you spend time alone with each other. You must be able to trust each other and feel safe when you are together.

Here are some things that can happen in a dating relationship that are unsafe and against the law:

> ➤ *Your date hits, shoves, or pushes you.*
> Hurting someone is never okay, even if the person who hurts you says "sorry" afterward. This is called *physical abuse,* and it is against the law. Many times people who hit or use violence say they are sorry. Then later, they hit again and say they are sorry. Then another time they might hit again and say they are sorry. Physical abuse is never okay and is a

good reason to break up the relationship. (See Chapter 8 about breaking up.)

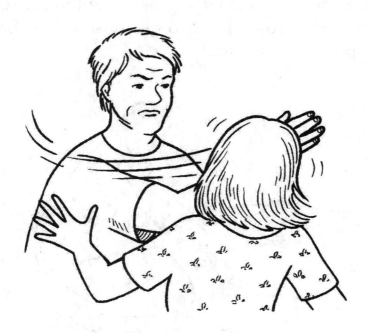

➤ *Your date forces you to do sexual things* like touching or looking at his or her private parts or having sex. Forcing someone to do sexual things they don't want to do is called *sexual assault*. Using force means pushing, grabbing, or holding someone down to make them do something. Sometimes the person also uses threats (saying things that make the other person feel afraid). Even if you are dating, it is not okay for your boyfriend or girlfriend to force you to do sexual things.

Sexual assault is against the law. It is wrong because the other person hasn't given permission. It is wrong because the person is afraid to say no. It is a good reason to break up a relationship.

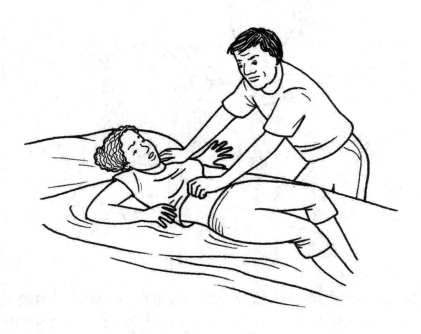

DATING

DETAIL

In healthy dating relationships, boyfriends and girlfriends never force each other to do things they don't want to do. Boundaries are respected.

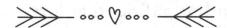

If your date tries to do any of these things to you, it means the relationship is unsafe and unhealthy. If he or she is in your home, ask him or her to leave, or use your phone to call for help. If your boyfriend/girlfriend does not leave, call 911. If you are away from home, leave if you can. Then use your cell phone to call an adult you trust.

You have the right to feel safe in boyfriend/girlfriend relationships. If you don't, that is a good reason to break up the relationship.

OTHER DANGER SIGNS

Here are some other signs that your relationship is in trouble. These things are not against the law, but they are signs of an unhealthy relationship.

➤ **One person has all the power and control in your relationship.**

For example, your boyfriend/girlfriend:
- gets to make all the decisions
- tells you how to act
- doesn't listen to how you feel
- tells you who you can spend your time with
- tells you how to live your life.

This could be a sign your relationship is unhealthy. If you feel like you have no power in your relationship, it is a good reason to break up the relationship.

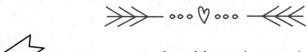

In healthy relationships, couples take turns making decisions. In healthy relationships, power is shared.

➤ *One person says hurtful things that make you feel bad about who you are.*

Using words to hurt people is called *verbal abuse.* It is not okay. Here are some examples of verbal abuse:

- "You're stupid!"
- "You're retarded!"
- "You're ugly!"
- "You're fat!"
- "Nobody else will ever go out with you!"
- "You'll never get a job!"

Words can hurt! If your boyfriend/girlfriend puts you down, it means he or she doesn't really care about you! Verbal abuse is never okay and is unhealthy. It is a good reason to break up the relationship.

➤ *There is pressure to do sexual things.*

Pressure means your date uses words to try to get you to do sexual things you don't want to do. Sometimes a boyfriend or girlfriend will pressure you by begging or lying. Sometimes he or she will use words that make you feel like you should give in. Here is what pressure sounds like:

- "If you loved me you would have sex with me."
- "I'll break up with you if you don't have sex with me."

- "Don't you care about me?"
- "This is what boyfriends/girlfriends do."
- "Come on...please?"

Using pressure to get what you want is not okay. You and your boyfriend/girlfriend have the right to make decisions without pressure.

➤ **The relationship feels rushed and is moving too fast.**

Sometimes one person in a relationship wants to get serious faster than the other person. After going on one or two dates, he or she might want to have sex, get engaged, or get married. This can feel too fast for many people. It can take a long time for two people to get to know each other. Relationships take time to grow and develop. Forcing people to do things too fast can feel unsafe.

 You have the right to feel safe with the person you are dating. If you believe your relationship is unhealthy, that is a good reason to break up.

ACTIVITY: IS YOUR RELATIONSHIP HEALTHY?

Below is a list of things that can happen if you are dating someone. Some of the things can help you to trust your date. Other things are warning signs that you should not trust your date. Look at the list and decide if these things are **T**rue or **F**alse about your boyfriend/girlfriend. If you are not sure how to answer, try doing this activity together with an adult you trust.

Healthy Behaviors 👍	T/F?	Unhealthy Behaviors 👎	T/F?
Your boyfriend/girlfriend calls often to see how you are doing.		Your boyfriend/girlfriend only calls when he/she needs something from you.	
Your date is easy to talk to. You can talk with each other about anything.		**You have to be careful what you say or do, or your date gets angry.**	
You can be open and honest with each other.		Your date lies to you about things (like where he or she lives or works).	
Your date is kind to you when you are alone and with others.		**Your date yells at you or says mean things when you are alone with him or her.**	

Healthy Behaviors 👍	T/F?	Unhealthy Behaviors 👎	T/F?
Your date enjoys spending time with your family and friends.		**Your date gets mad or jealous when you spend time with others.**	
Touch & affection boundaries are respected (your date stops when you say "stop").		**You feel pressure to change your touch and affection boundaries.**	
Your date is always there when you need help.		Your date doesn't seem to care or makes excuses when you need help.	
You have gotten to know your boyfriend/girlfriend slowly over time.		**Your relationship feels rushed and is moving too fast.**	
You take turns making decisions.		**Your boyfriend/ girlfriend has all the control.**	
You can be your true self when you are with your date.		**Your date is only interested in your body, not who you are as a person.**	
Your date makes you feel safe, happy and loved.		There is anger, fear, and jealousy in your relationship.	

Healthy Behaviors	T/F?	Unhealthy Behaviors	T/F?
You can rely (depend) on each other.		Your date makes many promises but never keeps them. (He or she is not dependable.)	
You respect each other's property.		Your date takes things without asking or keeps things that are yours.	
When there are problems, you work together to fix them.		**You fight a lot, and problems are never fixed.**	
Your boyfriend/ girlfriend shows affection in a loving, caring way.		**Your date has shoved, pushed, or hit you.**	

How did you do on the quiz?

You are probably in a *healthy relationship* if:

♥ you answered *true* to all or most of the statements in the first column

AND

♥ you answered *false* to all of the **bolded** statements in the second column.

You are probably in an **unhealthy relationship** if:

➤ you answered true to any of the bolded statements in the second column.

Remember, if you don't feel respected in your relationship, that is a good reason for you to break up. See the next chapter to find out how to end a relationship.

CHAPTER 8

Time to Break Up?

BREAKING UP

Breaking up means ending your relationship with your boyfriend or girlfriend. Couples break up when one or both people in the relationship decide they want to stop dating each other. Here are some common reasons couples break up:

➤ One person loses interest in keeping the relationship going.

➤ One person moves away, and it is too hard to keep the relationship going.

➤ The couple can't get along with each other.

➤ One person is just not happy in the relationship.

➤ Each person wants something different from the relationship.

➤ The relationship is not safe or it is unhealthy. (See Chapter 7.)

➤ The couple does not have anything (or enough) in common.

➤ One person in the relationship wants to date someone else.

HOW DO YOU BREAK UP?

1. First, ***think about the reasons you are not happy in the relationship.*** Write them down if that helps you remember. Or tell them to someone you trust so he or she can help you remember.

2. Next, **decide how you will tell your boyfriend/girlfriend.** If you are going to tell him or her in person, pick a place where you can talk in private. Breaking up with someone is private and very personal. If you do not feel safe when you are alone with the person, it is best to call or text him or her.

3. **Decide what you will say.** Make it clear that you are breaking up. You could say:

   - "I want to stop dating you."
   - "I don't want to be your boyfriend/ girlfriend anymore."
   - "I am breaking up with you."

4. Then **give a reason that is honest, but kind.** You could say:

   - "I don't think we are a good match for each other."
   - "It was fun, but we really don't have much in common."
   - "I just don't have time to be in a relationship right now."

5. **Practice what you will say** with a family or staff member so you are ready. Try role-playing the breakup so you know how it feels to say the words.

HANDLING YOUR GIRLFRIEND'S OR BOYFRIEND'S REACTION

You need to be ready for things that could happen after you tell the person you want to break up. For example:

➤ What if he or she begs you to stay boyfriend or girlfriend? (Answer: keep repeating your breakup message over and over.)

➤ What if the person keeps calling and texting after the breakup? (Answer: don't answer texts or calls. If you don't answer, the calls or texts will stop.)

➤ What if you see the person you broke up
with at other places? (Answer: say "hi"
but don't act like you are boyfriend and
girlfriend again.)

Hi! How are you?

I miss you!

Gotta go talk to my
friend…

Wanna slow dance?

How about a fast
dance instead?

HOW **NOT** TO BREAK UP

Breakups are always hard. They can be even harder if they are done the wrong way. Here are ways *not* to break up with someone:

➤ Do not use your Facebook (or other social media) page to send a breakup message. Breakups are private.

➤ Don't just ignore the person and pretend the relationship is over. If you want to break up, you need to let the person know. He or she has a right to know how you feel and what is going on.

➤ Do not ask a friend or parent to break up for you. This is not middle school. If you want to break up, *you* need to do the work.

➤ Do not go someplace fun and then break up at the *end* of the date. If you know you are not a good match, the sooner you tell him or her, the better.

IF SOMEONE BREAKS UP WITH YOU

When someone you really like breaks up with you, it hurts! Most people feel sad, angry, or lonely when a dating relationship stops. It is normal to feel this way.

Getting over a breakup can take time. Here are some ways to handle your feelings after a breakup with your boyfriend/girlfriend:

➤ Talk to a family member or friend about your feelings.

➤ Write about your feelings in a journal.

➤ Learn from your experience. Think about things that went wrong. Write down ideas for how to make your next dating relationship better.

➤ Do things you enjoy and that make you feel happy.

➤ Spend time with friends and family.

➤ Be active. Take a walk; get some exercise. Moving can take your mind off things.

Breakups are hard, but most people start to feel better over time.

CHAPTER 9

Time to Get More Serious?

This chapter covers the things you need to know if you are in a serious relationship.

If you are a good match for each other and have dated for a long time (many months or even years), you both might decide you are ready for a more serious relationship. Being in a serious relationship can mean many things. It can mean:

♥ Nothing changes. You just continue to enjoy dating only each other and nobody else.

♥ You are more comfortable with each other.

♥ You want to share touch and affection in more serious ways.

♥ You want to spend more time together.

♥ You want to plan a future together.

Serious relationships are for adults. If you are under eighteen, your parents still have the right to make decisions for you. They are your **guardians.** Some people over age eighteen also have guardians. If you have a guardian, it means you need help making decisions that affect your life in a big way. Serious relationships can affect your life in a big way.

Remember, a guardian's job is to make sure that decisions being made will make you and your life better. If you are your own guardian, this chapter will help you learn about the work involved in being in serious relationships.

If you are not sure if you are your own guardian, ask your parents or the people who support you.

THINKING ABOUT A FUTURE TOGETHER

When two people are in a serious relationship, they make a commitment to each other. This means you and your boyfriend/girlfriend are no longer interested in dating other people. The two of you only want to be with each other and nobody else.

Couples should only think about planning a future together if all of these things are true:

- ♥ Both people are sure they are a good match.

- ♥ They get along well.

- ♥ The relationship is healthy.

The next sections cover some questions that couples think about when they plan for a future together.

WHERE SHOULD YOU LIVE?

When boyfriends/girlfriends are very serious about each other, they often want to live together. They might be able to do this right away if they both have had experience living alone or with a roommate. But sometimes boyfriends/girlfriends need to learn some independent living skills first.

Living on Your Own

One way to learn new skills is to move into your own space. This will help you learn ways to take care of yourself and be independent. And you will find out what things you need help with.

It is important to know what you are able to do by yourself before you decide to live with your boyfriend/

girlfriend. Living on your own before you live with someone else is one way to learn skills that will help you live independently as a couple.

Living Together

Living together means you share the same living space with your boyfriend or girlfriend. Living together means you both cook, clean, and do other chores. It also means you both sleep in the same bed.

Living with someone can help you find out if you can still get along when you see each other all the time. It is also a way to find out what things you can manage on your own and what you need help with.

SHOULD YOU GET ENGAGED OR MARRIED?

Getting engaged means two people have decided they are going to be married in the future. You might get each other rings to show that you are engaged. You might set a date to be married, or you might decide on a date later. If you and your boyfriend/girlfriend are thinking about marriage, you need to talk to the people who support you.

Getting married is a legal ceremony. If you have a guardian, he or she may get to decide whether or not you can be married. That's because there are legal and financial issues that change after a couple gets married. For example, many adults with disabilities get money from the government to help them pay for rent, food, and medical care. This money may be reduced if you get married. For some couples, this might not matter. For other couples, it is a big deal.

Getting married is a way that couples tell the world that they have found a person to love and support forever. It means they each will have a husband or wife and will not date other people. It means they will live together as a couple and sleep in the same bed.

SHOULD YOU HAVE A COMMITMENT CEREMONY?

Instead of getting married, some couples decide to have a commitment ceremony. This is a ceremony to show the world they are committed to being together, only with each other. The ceremony can be very fancy, like a wedding, or it can be simple and quiet.

Having a commitment ceremony does not change the benefits you receive from the government. So, this is one way couples with disabilities can live like they are married and keep their government benefits.

IMPORTANT STEPS IN PLANNING YOUR FUTURE

If you and your boyfriend/girlfriend are interested in planning a future together, it is a good idea to:

➤ Talk with the people who support you. If you live at home, talk to your parents. If you live in the community, talk to staff. If you have a guardian, you may have to convince him or her that you are ready for a more serious relationship. He or she might want you to learn more skills or do other things to show you are ready. Remember, you may have to get your guardian's permission to marry and work with him or her to make a plan for your future.

➤ Get some help with a budget. Many of the choices you have will be based on what you both can afford.

➤ Become as independent as possible. Figure out what you need to learn and what skills you can work on. There is work involved in living on your own or with your boyfriend/ girlfriend. Learning how to do laundry, cook, clean, pay bills, and live on a budget can help you and your boyfriend or girlfriend be successful.

There are many responsibilities in serious relationships. It is helpful for couples to learn and talk about these responsibilities so they will know how to handle them.

SHARING TOUCH AND AFFECTION IN MORE SERIOUS WAYS

If you watch TV or use the Internet, it can **seem** like all people ever do is think about, talk about, or have sex. In the real world, it isn't usually like that. Yes, sharing touch and affection **is** a part of a healthy relationship, but every couple is different. Each couple gets to decide what kinds of touch and affection feel right for them. Chapter 4 showed pictures of ways couples who are just getting to know each other might share touch and affection.

When two people have been together for a while and care about each other very much, they sometimes agree they would like to share touch and affection in more serious ways. This usually means being naked together or having sex. Here are some important things to know and talk about with your boyfriend or girlfriend **before** you make that kind of decision:

♥ Is there a private place where you can be together? Having sex and being naked together is very private. Most couples have sex in their bedrooms with the door closed.

♥ Is this something **both of you** are sure you want to do?

♥ How will you avoid an unwanted pregnancy?

♥ How will you protect each other from sexually transmitted diseases?

Consent—Are there Two Yeses?

On page 46 we talked about boundaries and how they can be different for each person. If you and your boyfriend/girlfriend are thinking about having sex with each other, each of you must **decide for yourself** if you want to have sex. This means all of these things are true:

1. There is no pressure from your boyfriend or girlfriend (see page 48).

2. There are no bribes or threats (see page 48).

3. Your boyfriend/girlfriend is not forcing you to have sex (see page 67).

Consenting to sex means both of these things are true:

1. You have the information you need to decide whether to have sex.

2. You are making the decision on your own.

The same is true for your boyfriend or girlfriend. Each person in the relationship gets to decide what feels right for him or her.

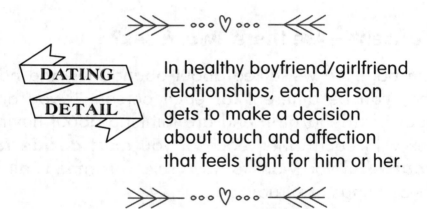

In healthy boyfriend/girlfriend relationships, each person gets to make a decision about touch and affection that feels right for him or her.

CONSENT TO SEX = 2 CONFIDENT YESES

Each of you has the right to change your mind at any time. It is important for each couple to make a decision that feels right for them.

What Is Sex?

There are many ways to have sex, but most of them involve sharing your body in very private ways. When couples are naked together, here are some things that they might do:

♥   take a bath or shower together

♥   massage each other's bodies with lotion

♥   kiss, hug, and cuddle

♥   gently touch each other's bodies in places they each like to be touched

♥   touch or gently massage each other's private parts (penis, clitoris, nipples) with the hands or mouth

These activities can help a couple get ready for sex if that is what they want. A man's body might be ready for sex when his penis is stiff and hard (this is called an **erection**). A woman's body might be ready for sex when her vagina becomes wet and slippery. When these things happen to both partners, they may want to have sex.

How Does a Woman Get Pregnant?

If you both decide you want to have sex, it is very important to understand how women get pregnant. You do not want to accidentally create a baby if you and your boyfriend/girlfriend are not ready for one!

In order for a woman to get pregnant, sperm from the man's body must join with an egg from the woman's body.

Let's review how a sperm and an egg might join together during sex.

- ♥ During sex, if they are both ready, the man puts his penis inside of a woman's vagina.

- ♥ The man and woman move together for a while. Then, with his penis still inside of the woman, the man squirts a liquid that has sperm into the woman's vagina. (This is called "coming" or "ejaculating.")

- ♥ The sperm find their way inside of the woman. They swim into her uterus and toward the ovaries.

- ♥ If the timing is right, a sperm might meet up with an egg that is coming out of the woman's ovary. If the sperm and egg join, the egg is fertilized.

♥ The fertilized egg moves into the woman's uterus. There it attaches to the wall of the uterus.

♥ The egg will stay and grow until it is a baby inside the uterus. This takes about nine months.

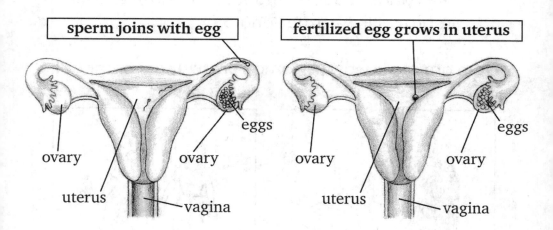

A woman doesn't get pregnant every time she has sex. A sperm has to find an egg that is ready to be fertilized. But every time a woman has sex with a man without using birth control, there is a chance she will get pregnant. (See the information about birth control on page 101.)

If you did not learn about sex and pregnancy at school or have forgotten the details, it would be an excellent idea to take a sex education class. You can also find good information in books.

For more information about body parts, sex, and reproduction, you may want to look at these websites:

♥ www.woodbinehouse.com/
boyfriends&girlfriends.asp

♥ www.plannedparenthood.org/learn/sexuality/
reproductive-sexual-anatomy

Here are some ways a woman **cannot** get pregnant:

Protecting Each Other from Unwanted Pregnancy & STIs

Let's say that you have both decided you are ready to have sex. (There is a confident yes from each of you.) If so, you will need to learn about birth control. You can go to your doctor or a family planning clinic to learn about this together.

Birth control is something a man or woman can use when they want to have sex, but do not want to make a baby or get a sexually transmitted infection (STI). An STI is an infection you get from having sex with someone who already has an STI.

There are many kinds of birth control. Your doctor or health care provider can help you decide what type of birth control might work best for you. Some birth

Couples should use birth control if they want to have sex with each other but do not want to make a baby or get a sexually transmitted infection. Your doctor or health care provider can help you decide what birth control method might work best for you.

control methods are medical devices. If you have a guardian, you will need his or her help. He or she can help you decide on a method that will work best.

CONCLUSION

Being in a boyfriend/girlfriend relationship can be exciting and fun...but it can be hard work too!

For most people, it takes time and practice to learn all of the things this book talks about. If you need help, talk to another person you live with or trust. That way you can be safe and have fun!

Dating Dilemmas

Sometimes it can be hard to figure out what to do when you are in a dating relationship or trying to start one. This section includes some common dating problems that people run into. Decide how you would solve each problem. Then turn to page 107 to see if you picked the best answer.

Hint: some of these dating dilemmas have more than one right answer.

A. I really like someone, but I'm not sure the other person likes me. Should I:
1. Give the person a hug or kiss to show I'm interested.
2. Send signals that I am interested (flirt) and pay close attention to the signals the person sends back.

3. Call the person my boyfriend/girlfriend, and then he or she will *have* to like me.
4. Ask the person if he or she wants to be my boyfriend/girlfriend.

B. I really like someone who is already dating somebody else. I could:

1. Enjoy my sexual feelings when I am around this person, but keep them to myself.
2. Let the person know I like him or her by hugging or kissing him or her.
3. Send signals that I am interested (flirt) and pay attention to the signals the person sends back (see page 26).
4. Try to break up the relationship so I can date the person.

C. Someone I know acts like we are dating each other, but we are just friends and not in a boyfriend/girlfriend relationship. I could:

1. Act like we are boyfriend/girlfriend (kiss, hug, flirt, etc.) even though I'm not interested.
2. Pretend I like the person so he/she doesn't feel bad.
3. Remind the person nicely that we are not boyfriend/girlfriend, just friends. If the

person tries to kiss me, stop him or her
and say, "We're just friends, remember?"
4. Have my parents/staff take care of the
problem.

**D. My parents/staff are afraid to let me
date. They are afraid someone will take
advantage of me. Should I:**
1. Find someone to date but keep it a secret
so they won't know.
2. Learn about my rights and responsibilities
of being in a dating relationship.
3. Talk to my parents/staff about what I
want.
4. Take a class about dating so I am
prepared.

**E. My friends all have boyfriends/girlfriends,
but I feel too shy to ask anyone out. I would
feel really bad if I asked someone out and
the person said no. I can:**
1. Skip the whole dating scene.
2. Wait until someone is interested in me
and asks me out.
3. Be brave, ask someone out, and know
that it's okay if he or she says no.
4. Have my staff or parents set me up with
someone.

F. ***My boyfriend/girlfriend and I want to share more touch and affection, but we never get any privacy. We can:***

    1. Talk to the people we live with about what we both want.
    2. Find a place in the community where we can be in private.
    3. Share private touch and affection in public (in front of others) and hope people leave or don't notice.
    4. Just show our affection in acceptable ways in public.

G. ***My boyfriend/girlfriend is really nice to me when others are around but not very nice when we are alone. I could:***

    1. Stay with him/her because having a mean boyfriend/girlfriend is better than having nobody at all.
    2. Make sure I have a chaperone or only go on double dates so I am never alone with him/her.
    3. Talk to my boyfriend/girlfriend about the problem and see if things get better (see page 60 for how to fix problems).
    4. Break up! I have the right to feel respected in my dating relationships (see pages 46-47).

H. I think I might be gay. How can I find out for sure?

1. Ask my friends if they think I'm gay.
2. Look at myself in the mirror and see if I look gay.
3. Pay attention to my sexual feelings and see if I have more crushes on men or women.
4. Talk to a person I trust about what I am feeling.

ANSWER KEY: DATING DILEMMAS

A. I really like someone, but I'm not sure the other person likes me.

Best Answer: 2. If you're not sure if someone likes you, it's best to send some signals and see what the person does. Hugging or kissing people you have a crush on is not okay. And acting like someone is your boyfriend or girlfriend when they are not can embarrass the person and blow your chances. See page 26 for tips on sending and reading signals.

B. I really like someone who is already dating somebody else.

Best Answer: 1. If someone you like is already in a boyfriend/girlfriend relationship, the person is not available. In order to start a relationship, both people have to be single. You have a few choices. You could wait and see if the relationship stops at some time in the future. Or, try looking for someone else who is single. It is *not okay* to act like someone is your boyfriend/girlfriend when he or she is not.

C. Someone I know acts like we are dating each other, but we are just friends and not in a boyfriend/girlfriend relationship.

Best Answer: 3. It is always best to be honest. Remember, in order for a boyfriend/girlfriend relationship to start, both people should be interested in each other. It is *not okay* to act like you are someone's boyfriend/girlfriend when you are not. Stand up for yourself and let the person know how you feel.

D. My parents/staff are afraid to let me date. They are afraid someone will take advantage of me.

Best Answers: 2 or 4. Learning about dating, especially if you are new at this, is always a good thing. Get information from a class, from this book, or on your own. That can help you know what to expect, so you can be ready. **AND 3.** Part of being ready to date and growing up is learning how to speak up for yourself and tell other people how you feel and what you want. Knowing how to let others know what you want and then standing up for yourself is called being a *self-advocate*. Knowing how to be a self-advocate is a good skill to have in boyfriend/girlfriend relationships!

E. My friends all have boyfriends/girlfriends, but I feel too shy to ask anyone out. I would feel really bad if I asked someone out and the person said no.

Best Answer: It depends. The answer to this dilemma depends on how badly you want a boyfriend or girlfriend. If it doesn't matter that much to you, then **Answers 1 or 2** make sense. If you really, really want to date but are too shy, then **Answer 3** might work better. If you're shy, try practicing what you could say in a mirror. See pages 32-35 for ways to ask someone out on a date. If you never ask, you'll never know if the person might feel the same way! And remember: being rejected now and then is part of dating.

F. My boyfriend/girlfriend and I want to share touch and affection, but we never get any privacy.

Best Answer: 1. This is another time when you might need to stand up for yourself and tell the people in your life what you want. If you live with staff or your parents, they may be worried about your safety or your partner's safety. Or they may worry that you or your date might get pregnant. So, you may need to convince them that:

1. you and your date both know how to handle yourselves when you are alone together and

2. you know how to use birth control.

Talk to them about what you know and how you feel. Then ask them what else they think you need to know.

G. My boyfriend/girlfriend is really nice to me when others are around but not very nice when we are alone.

Best Answer: Start with 3: If there is a problem, it is good to share your feelings and talk about what you want, then see if it things get better. If your boyfriend or girlfriend does not listen, or does not change his/

her behavior, then you may need to **move to Answer 4.** Remember, how a person treats you when you are alone helps you know what kind of person he or she really is. If your boyfriend/girlfriend does or says mean things when you are alone, it is also a sign the relationship is unhealthy. (See page 66 to review signs of a healthy and unhealthy relationship.) You have the right to feel safe and respected in your boyfriend/girlfriend relationship.

H. I think I might be gay. How can I find out for sure?

Best Answer: Start with 3. It isn't always easy to figure out if you are gay (only getting crushes on or wanting to date people of your same sex) or straight (only getting crushes on or wanting to date people of the opposite sex). Some people who are gay know early on. For others, it can take time to figure things out. It's important to know that daydreaming or wondering what it would be like to touch or kiss someone who is the same sex as you does not necessarily mean you are gay. And having one sexual experience with someone of your same sex doesn't necessarily mean you are gay either. Start by paying close attention to your sexual feelings and who you are attracted to. If you think you might be gay it can helpful to do **4.** Talk to a professional or an adult you trust about your questions or concerns.

Online Dating Sites

Here are a couple of websites where it may be safe to "meet" other people with disabilities who are looking for someone to date. If you use these sites, be sure that you do not share personal information with strangers you meet online. For example, do not give your address, phone number, birth date, or Social Security number to someone you do not know. As Chapter 3 explains, when you are looking for someone to date, it is usually better to meet people in person.

♥ For people on the autism spectrum:
   https://www.spectrumsingles.com/

♥ For people with intellectual disabilities:
   http://www.specialbridge.com/

Index

About the Author

Terri Couwenhoven is a sexuality educator who works with people who have intellectual disabilities. She is the Clinic Coordinator for the Down Syndrome Clinic of Wisconsin at Children's Hospital of Wisconsin.

She is also the author of *Teaching Children with Down Syndrome about Their Bodies, Boundaries, and Sexuality*, *The Boys Guide to Growing Up*, and *The Girls' Guide to Growing Up*.